Saint Therese

Novena and Prayers

By
Mary Mark Wickenhiser, FSP

Pauline
BOOKS & MEDIA
Boston

Nihil Obstat: Rev. Thomas W. Buckley, STD, SSL

Imprimatur: ✠ Most Rev. Seán O'Malley, O.F.M. Cap.
Archbishop of Boston
June 14, 2004

ISBN 0-8198-7089-7

Cover art: Tracy L. Christianson

Texts of the New Testament used in this work are taken from *The New Testament: St. Paul Catholic Edition*, translated by Mark A. Wauck, copyright © 2000, Society of St. Paul, Staten Island, New York, and used by permission. All rights reserved.

Texts of the Psalms used in this work are translated by Manuel Miguens. Copyright © 1995, Daughters of St. Paul.

"P" and PAULINE are registered trademarks of the Daughters of St. Paul

Published by Pauline Books & Media, 50 Saint Paul's Avenue, Boston MA 02130-3491. www.pauline.org.

Printed in the U.S.A.

Pauline Books & Media is the publishing house of the Daughters of St. Paul, an international congregation of women religious serving the Church with the communications media.

5 6 7 8 9 10   23 22 21 20 19

Contents

What Is a Novena?

The Catholic tradition of praying novenas has its roots in the earliest days of the Church. In the Acts of the Apostles we read that after the ascension of Jesus, the apostles returned to Jerusalem, to the upper room, where "They all devoted themselves single-mindedly to prayer, along with some women and Mary the Mother of Jesus and his brothers" (Acts 1:14). Jesus had instructed his disciples to wait for the coming of the Holy Spirit, and on the day of Pentecost, the Spirit of the Lord came to them. This prayer of the first Christian community was the first "novena." Based on this, Christians have always prayed for various needs, trusting that God both hears and answers prayer.

The word "novena" is derived from the Latin term *novem*, meaning nine. In biblical times numbers held deep symbolism for people. The number "three," for example, symbolized perfection, fullness, completeness. The number nine—three times three—symbolized perfection times perfection. Novenas developed because it was thought that—symbolically speaking—nine days represented the perfect amount of time to pray. The ancient Greeks and Romans had the custom of mourning for nine days after a death. The early Christian Church offered Mass for the deceased for nine consecutive days. During the Middle Ages novenas in preparation for solemn feasts became popular, as did novenas to particular saints.

Whether a novena is made solemnly—in a parish church in preparation for a feastday—or in the privacy of one's home, as Christians we never really pray alone. Through the waters of Baptism we have become members of the Body of Christ and are thereby united to every other member of Christ's Mystical Body. When we pray, we are spiritually united with all the other members.

Just as we pray for each other while here on earth, those who have gone before us and are united with God in heaven can pray for us and intercede for us as well. We Catholics use the term "communion of saints" to refer to this exchange of spiritual help among the members of the Church on earth, those who have died and are being purified, and the saints in heaven.

While nothing can replace the celebration of Mass and the sacraments as the Church's highest form of prayer, devotions have a special place in

Catholic life. Devotions such as the Stations of the Cross can help us enter into the sufferings of Jesus and give us an understanding of his personal love for us. The mysteries of the rosary can draw us into meditating on the lives of Jesus and Mary. Devotions to the saints can help us witness to our faith and encourage us in our commitment to lead lives of holiness and service as they did.

———————— ❧ ————————

How to use this booklet

*T*he morning and evening prayers are modeled on the Liturgy of the Hours, following its pattern of psalms, scripture readings, and intercessions.

We suggest that during the novena you make time in your schedule to pray the morning prayer and evening prayer. If you are able, try to also set aside a time during the day when you can pray the novena and any other particular prayer(s) you have chosen. Or you can recite the devotional prayers at the conclusion of the morning or evening prayer. What is important is to pray with expectant faith and confidence in a loving God who will answer our prayers in the way that will most benefit us. The Lord "satisfies the thirsty, and the hungry he fills with good things" (Ps 107:9).

St. Thérèse

Patroness of Missionaries and the Missions, Protector of AIDS and Tuberculosis Patients, Guardian of Those Who Follow Her "Little Way"

When Thérèse was born at Alencon, France, on January 2, 1873, no one could have dreamed her life would prove so remarkable. For she seemed unremarkable in every way. She was the youngest of five girls born to Louis and Zelie Martin, who were ordinary, hardworking people. Her devoutly Catholic parents raised their children with great love. But tragedy soon struck their happy family. When Thérèse was only four years old, Zelie Martin died of breast cancer. This came as a deep blow to the little girl. Bereft of her mother, she grew deeply attached to her older sister, Pauline.

Despite this great loss, Thérèse showed an unusual degree of spiritual maturity. But she later admitted that she had a certain emotional weakness, probably made worse by her mother's death. As a young girl she was quite sensitive and the least thing could cause her an emotional upset. On the feast of Christmas, 1886, however, Thérèse received a special grace, which she called her "complete conversion." A seemingly insignificant action of her father occasioned it. He was tired after midnight Mass and grew annoyed with the childish way Thérèse was fussing over her Christmas presents. Normally such an incident would have upset her to the point of tears, but suddenly, she saw it all in a completely different way. Instead of reacting with tears, she overcame her sensitivity and acted with a newfound emotional maturity. Thérèse recognized this as the work of grace. Years later she said that what she had tried in vain to do for so long, Jesus did for her in an instant.

Thérèse reflected on these ordinary experiences, things which happen to everyone, and searched their depths for the grace that God gave her through them. She put this wisdom into her autobiography, *The Story of a Soul*. This book, along with some letters and recorded conversations, became her spiritual testament. She called it her "little way," the way of love, because everyone could follow it. Everyone can love, so everyone can become a saint.

To the casual observer it would seem that Thérèse lived an ordinary life. At the age of fifteen she entered the Carmel at Lisieux, following her two sisters, Pauline and Marie. She lived like all the other nuns, but deep within her soul an extraordinary work of grace was going on.

Moved by divine love, she offered her life to God as a sacrificial gift on June 9, 1895. Shortly afterward she grew ill with tuberculosis, a deadly disease in those days. At the same time, she suffered another, greater trial: spiritual darkness. Devoid of all spiritual consolation, she had nothing left but sheer faith in God. Thérèse suffered this trial until she died on September 30, 1897, at the age of twenty-four.

On May 17, 1925, Pope Pius XI canonized her, and in 1927, he made her patroness of the missions. Her spiritual teaching continued to grow in popularity and spread around the world. On October 19, 1997, Pope John Paul II proclaimed her a Doctor of the Church. In his apostolic letter, *The Science of Divine Love,* he wrote of Thérèse: "In her life God has offered the world a precise message, indicating an evangelical way, the 'little way,' which everyone can take.... The core of her message is actually the mystery itself of God-Love, of the Triune God, infinitely perfect in himself."

Marianne Lorraine Trouvé, FSP

Morning Prayer

*M*orning prayer is a time to give praise and thanks to God, to remind ourselves that he is the source of all beauty and goodness. Lifting one's heart and mind to God in the early hours of the day puts one's life into perspective: God is our loving Creator who watches over us with tenderness and is always ready to embrace us with his compassion and mercy.

While at prayer, try to create a prayerful atmosphere, perhaps with a burning candle to remind you that Christ is the light who illumines your daily path, an open Bible to remind you that the Lord is always present, a crucifix to remind you of the depths of God's love for you. Soft music can also contribute to a serene and prayerful mood.

If a quiet place is not available, or if you pray as you commute to and from work, remember that the God who loves you is present everywhere and hears your prayer no matter the setting.

It is good to give thanks and praise to the Lord our God,
and proclaim his love in the morning.
Glory to the Father, and to the Son, and to the
     Holy Spirit,
as it was in the beginning, is now, and will be
     forever. Amen.

Psalm 8

The heavens and the earth proclaim God's glory.

O LORD our God,
how majestic is your name over all the earth!
Your praise resounds above the heavens.
Out of the mouths of babes and infants,
you have found praise to thwart your foes,
to silence the rebel and the enemy.
When I contemplate your heavens, the work of
     your hands,
the moon and the stars, which you established;
what are human beings that you should be mindful
     of us—
that you should care for us?
Still, you have made us little less than the gods
and crowned us with glory and splendor.
You have given us dominion over the works of
     your hands;

you have put all things under our feet:
O LORD our God,
how majestic is your name over all the earth!

The Word of God
Matthew 18:1–5

The way of spiritual childhood is the way of humility, the way of love. Living the "little way" means recognizing one's nothingness, expecting everything from God, just as a little child expects everything from its father.

At that time the disciples came to Jesus and said, "Who is the greatest in the Kingdom of Heaven?" He called a child forward, stood it before them, and said, "Amen, I say to you, unless you turn about and become like children, you will not enter the Kingdom of Heaven! Therefore, whoever humbles himself like this child, he is the greatest in the Kingdom of Heaven. And whoever receives one such child in my name, receives me."

I trust in the Lord. I rely on God's word.

From prayer one draws the strength needed to meet the challenges of daily life as a committed follower of Jesus Christ, and, as such, to be a living sign of the Lord's loving presence in the world.

Intercessions

Lord, I thank you for having gifted me with a new day. With joy in your loving presence and trust in your promise to care for all our needs, I place my petitions before you and pray:

Response: Lord, lead me in your love.

Open the eyes of my heart that I may recognize your loving Providence at work in the events of this day. **R.**

Help me to use my gifts and talents to generously serve the needs of others today. **R.**

Teach me how to be a loving person in all the ordinary events of my life. **R.**

Grant that all in my family may live in harmony with one another today. **R.**

(Add your own general intentions and your particular intentions for this novena.)

Conclude your intercessions by praying to our Heavenly Father in the words Jesus taught us:

Our Father, who art in heaven, hallowed be thy name; thy kingdom come; thy will be done on earth as it is in heaven. Give us this day our daily bread, and forgive us our trespasses, as we forgive those who trespass against us, and lead us not into temptation, but deliver us from evil. Amen.

Closing Prayer

*H*eavenly Father, hear my morning prayer. As I begin this day in dedication to you, let the splendor of your love light my way. Grant that I may live this day in joy of spirit and free from all sin. I ask this through Christ, your Son. Amen.

Let us praise the Lord.
And give him thanks.

Novena to St. Thérèse

"Everyone will see that everything comes from God.
Any glory that I shall have will be a gratuitous gift
from God and will not belong to me."*

(Place the intention for your novena.)

---

*E*ternal Father, in heaven you crown the merits
of all those who faithfully serve you in this life.
For the sake of the love which St. Thérèse had for
you, hear the petitions which she offers you on my
behalf; through her intercession hear and answer
my prayer.

Our Father, Hail Mary, Glory to the Father...

---

*The thoughts of St. Thérèse are taken from Don Mullan, ed.,
A Little Book of Thérèse of Lisieux (Boston: Pauline Books &
Media, 2002).

*E*ternal Son of God, you promised to reward the smallest service done to you in the person of our neighbor. Look with love on your servant St. Thérèse who ever had at heart the salvation of all people. For the sake of all she suffered here on earth, let her now spend her time in heaven doing good upon earth; through her intercession hear and answer my prayer.

Our Father, Hail Mary, Glory to the Father...

---

*E*ternal Holy Spirit, you gave St. Thérèse many spiritual gifts, and she opened her heart to receive them with love. For the sake of her faithfulness to the graces you gave her, listen to the prayers she offers you on my behalf and let fall from heaven a shower of roses. Through her intercession hear and answer my prayer.

Our Father, Hail Mary, Glory to the Father...

Our Father, who art in heaven, hallowed be thy name; thy kingdom come; thy will be done on earth as it is in heaven. Give us this day our daily bread, and forgive us our trespasses, as we forgive those who trespass against us, and lead us not into temptation, but deliver us from evil. Amen.

Hail Mary, full of grace, the Lord is with you. Blessed are you among women, and blessed is the fruit of your womb, Jesus. Holy Mary, Mother of God, pray for us sinners, now and at the hour of our death. Amen.

Glory to the Father, and to the Son, and to the Holy Spirit, as it was in the beginning, is now, and will be forever. Amen.

Prayers for Various Needs

Prayer for a Special Intention

*"I am a little brush that Jesus has chosen
in order to paint his own image
in the souls entrusted to my care."*

St. Thérèse, during your short life on earth you became a model of spiritual transparency, of love strong as death, and of wholehearted abandonment to God. Now, from heaven, ask these same spiritual gifts for me and the special intention I place in your care *(mention your request)*. Present my petition to Mary, Queen of Heaven, for I trust that in her motherly affection she will bring my request to her Son, Jesus. I ask this and all spiritual blessings, in the name of the Father, and of the Son, and of the Holy Spirit. Amen.

Our Father, Hail Mary, Glory to the Father…

Prayer to Live in God's Love

*"My only peace, my only happiness,
my only love is you, Lord!"*

St. Thérèse, model of the hidden life, I thank you for showing us that extraordinary deeds, miracles, and ecstasies are not needed to lead a life of holiness. I thank you for choosing to walk the "little way," which is possible for everyone. My life is ordinary, filled with routine duties that are often tedious and wearisome. Yet I know that these everyday tasks have great value in the eyes of God when done for love of him. I do not ask to spend my energies by performing extraordinary deeds or carrying out great works; I only ask that I may do whatever work God has given me to do in this life, be it ever so ordinary, in the spirit in which you went about your quiet life at Carmel. Saint of the "little way," ask the Lord to accept the offering of my heart that I, too, might do ordinary things with an extraordinary love, and that I may do whatever God asks of me only because I love him and because I am doing it for him. Safeguard those whom I love and those for whom I pray this day. I ask this and all things through Jesus Christ. Amen.

(adapted from common sources)

Prayer for Help in Time of Need

*"I find that trials help us to detach ourselves
from the earth; they make us look higher
than this world."*

St. Thérèse, radiant flower that flourished in the garden of Carmel, I thank you for the love of God and concern for humanity which led you to embrace a life of prayer and penance. How deep a debt of gratitude I owe you for the graces you have already obtained for me and for the world. I ask you now, once again, to intercede for me in my time of need that the Lord may grant the grace I now ask *(mention your request)*. Watch over me that I may grow in holiness; protect those whom I love and those for whom I pray. Trusting in Jesus' promise that whatever is asked in his name will be granted, I praise and thank God for his generous love, and I look to the day when I can glorify him with you and all the saints in heaven. Amen.

Our Father, Hail Mary, Glory to the Father…

Prayer for the Needs of the Church

"…in the heart of the Church, my mother,
I shall be love. Thus I shall be everything,
and thus my dream will be realized."

St. Thérèse, while on earth your desire was to live for Jesus alone, to undergo suffering for his sake, to make his Gospel message better known, and to make him loved by all. Now from heaven continue to send upon the world a shower of roses, spiritual favors that will inspire all persons to know that the passing things of this world cannot compare to the joys that await us in heaven.

For the Pope, ask the Lord to grant him the grace he needs to govern the Church with wisdom and love. For the bishops, obtain for them the spiritual gifts necessary to be true shepherds of the flocks given to their care. For priests, ask God to give them the courage they need to meet the challenges of their vocation. For men and women religious, ask that they be granted enthusiasm for their calling and a loving reverence for all those whom they serve in their varied ministries. For the laity in the Church, ask for the gift of fidelity to Christ and to their call to discipleship. For those who have distanced themselves from the Church, inspire them to undertake the interior journey that will lead them back to the grace of the sacraments. For all

Christians, ask for the gift of unity, and ask the Holy Spirit to inspire the hearts of all people to continue the saving work of Christ until the end of time when we will all be united in heaven. Amen.

(adapted from common sources)

Prayer for Holiness of Life

"Jesus wants to possess your heart completely. He wants you to be a great saint."

St. Thérèse, the Church has raised you up as a model and a witness to holiness of life as a reminder of our own destiny. I ask you to be a friend and guide to me as I follow the Lord's way and do my best to draw others to his love. Teach me how to be selfless and humble so that I may know the freedom of God's love and find joy in serving others rather than being served. Assist me in times of temptation; protect me from the Evil One. If I grow weary along my journey to heaven, remind me of my call to holiness and the reward of everlasting life promised to those who follow the Lord wholeheartedly. Amen.

Our Father, Hail Mary, Glory to the Father...

Prayer for Healing

"Above the clouds the sky is always blue."

Almighty and eternal God, healer of those who trust in you, through the intercession of St. Thérèse of the Child Jesus, hear my prayer for *(name)*. In your tender mercy, restore her/him to spiritual and/or bodily health that she/he may give you thanks, praise your name, and proclaim your wondrous love to all. I ask this through Christ your Son, our Lord. Amen.

Prayer for Families

"The good God gave me a father and mother more worthy of heaven than of earth."

St. Thérèse, Little Flower of Jesus, by the memory of the love your parents had for you, and the affectionate care of your sisters, obtain for my family and for those of the entire world the blessings of a loving and secure home-life. Ask the Lord to fill parents with a spirit of devotion and self-sacrifice, and children with obedient love, so that all homes may be like the home of Nazareth. Safeguard all families; assist those in difficult situations. Inspire a spirit of forgiveness and reconciliation among members of families plagued by anger and resentment. May the Holy Spirit pour out his light and love so that every family may be a reflection of the Holy Family. Amen.

(adapted from common sources)

Prayer for Missionaries

"...a soul that is burning with love cannot remain inactive. To love is to give everything. It is to give oneself."

St. Thérèse of the Child Jesus, although you never left the seclusion of Carmel you have been proclaimed the patroness of Catholic missions throughout the world. By the grace of the burning desire you had to preach the Gospel to the ends of the earth, I ask you to safeguard all missionaries. Ask the Lord to grant them courage and strength in the face of adversity, wisdom and zeal in proclaiming God's name among the nations, and fidelity and joy as his heralds of truth. Amen.

(adapted from common sources)

Prayer of Praise and Thanksgiving

It is fitting for us to praise and thank God for the graces and privileges he has bestowed upon the saints. Devotees of St. Thérèse may pray the following act of thanksgiving during their novena.

Lord Jesus, I praise, glorify, and bless you for all the graces and privileges you have bestowed upon your chosen servant, St. Thérèse of Lisieux. By her merits grant me your grace, and through her intercession help me in all my needs. At the hour of my death be with me until that time when I can join the saints in heaven to praise you forever and ever. Amen.

Litany in Honor of St. Thérèse

(For private use)

Lord, *have mercy on us.*
Christ, *have mercy on us.*
Lord, *have mercy on us.*
Christ, *hear us.*
Christ, *graciously hear us.*

God, the Father of heaven, *have mercy on us.*

God, the Son, Redeemer of the world,
have mercy on us.
God, the Holy Spirit, *R.*

Holy Mary, Mother of God, *pray for us.*

St. Thérèse of the Child Jesus, *pray for us.*
St. Thérèse of the Holy Face, *pray for us.*
St. Thérèse, child of Mary, *pray for us.*
St. Thérèse, devotee of St. Joseph, *pray for us.*
St. Thérèse, model for religious, *pray for us.*
St. Thérèse, flower of Carmel, *pray for us.*
St. Thérèse, help for the distressed, *pray for us.*
St. Thérèse, filled with love for the Blessed
    Sacrament, *pray for us.*
St. Thérèse, filled with the zeal of an apostle,
    pray for us.
St. Thérèse, filled with loyalty and love for the
    Holy Father, *pray for us.*
St. Thérèse, filled with the desire to be love in the
    heart of the Church, *pray for us.*
St. Thérèse, filled with extraordinary love for God
    and neighbor, *pray for us.*
St. Thérèse, filled with a heavenly flame of love,
    pray for us.
St. Thérèse, patient in sufferings, *pray for us.*

St. Thérèse, example of humility, *pray for us.*

St. Thérèse, who died for Love, *pray for us.*

St. Thérèse, who prayed for hardened sinners,
pray for us.

St. Thérèse, who desired to be as a little child,
pray for us.

St. Thérèse, who taught the way of spiritual
childhood, *pray for us.*

St. Thérèse, who taught us a childlike trust in
God, *pray for us.*

St. Thérèse, whom Jesus filled with a love for the
cross, *pray for us.*

St. Thérèse, who achieved holiness by doing
ordinary things with great love, *pray for us.*

St. Thérèse, who always said "yes" to God, *pray for us.*

St. Thérèse, who understood the spiritual value of
suffering, *pray for us.*

St. Thérèse, who offered your life to God for
priests and missionaries, *pray for us.*

St. Thérèse, who, through prayer, gained countless
souls for Christ, *pray for us.*

St. Thérèse, who promised to let fall a continual
shower of roses upon earth, *pray for us.*

St. Thérèse, who promised to spend your heaven
doing good upon earth, *pray for us.*

Lamb of God, you take away the sins of the world,
spare us, O Lord.
Lamb of God, you take away the sins of the world,
graciously hear us, O Lord.
Lamb of God, you take away the sins of the world,
have mercy on us.

V. Pray for us, St. Thérèse of the Child Jesus.
R. That we may become worthy of the promises of
Christ.

Let us pray.

*H*eavenly Father, you promised that those
who are willing to become like little children would enter your kingdom. Help us to follow in the footsteps of St. Thérèse with humility of heart and simplicity of life that we may obtain an everlasting reward in heaven. Grant this through Christ your Son. Amen.

(adapted from common sources)

Evening Prayer

As this day draws to a close we place ourselves in an attitude of thanksgiving. We take time to express our gratitude to a loving God for his abiding presence. We thank him for the gift of the day and all it brought with it. We thank him for all the things we were able to achieve throughout the day, and we entrust to him the concerns we have for tomorrow.

From the rising to the setting of the sun,
may the name of the Lord be praised.
Glory to the Father, and to the Son, and to the
    Holy Spirit,
as it was in the beginning, is now, and will be
    forever. Amen.

Take a few moments for a brief examination of conscience. Reflect on the ways God acted in your life today; how you responded to his invitations to think, speak, and act in a more Christ-like manner; and in what ways you would like to be a more faithful disciple tomorrow.

To you, Lord, I pray for mercy.
For the times I was harsh and insensitive in word
    or action.
To you, Lord, I pray for mercy.
For the times I was untruthful or unforgiving.
To you, Lord, I pray for mercy.
For the times I turned away from doing acts of
    kindness.
To you, Lord, I pray for mercy.
For the times… (any other petitions for pardon).

(Or any other Act of Sorrow.)

Psalm 100

Let all who live praise God.

Shout for joy to the LORD, all the earth.
Serve the LORD with gladness,
come before him with joyful song.
Know that the LORD is God.
He made us, we belong to him.
We are God's people and the flock that he
    pastures.
Enter his gates with thanksgiving,
enter his courts with songs of praise.

Give thanks to him and bless his name,
for the LORD is good, his loving kindness is everlasting,
his faithfulness endures through all generations.

Glory to the Father…

Psalm 62

God is my refuge and my strength.

My soul, silently trust in God alone,
for it is from him that I draw my hope.
He alone is my rock, my stronghold, and my salvation
—my fortress. I shall not waver.
My salvation and glory rest on God;
the stronghold that protects me
and my sanctuary is in God.
Trust in him, you people, whatever the times,
pour out your hearts in the presence of the LORD.
God is a refuge for us.
Yours, O LORD, is loving kindness;
for you repay every person according to their
  deeds.

Glory to the Father…

The Word of God
Matthew 6:19–21

God is the One to whom we can always turn in trust. What is of this earth will not last. Only God endures forever, and his eternal reward for those who love him will surpass our greatest hopes.

Do not store up treasures for yourselves on earth,
where moth and rust destroy,
and where thieves break in and steal.
Store up treasures for yourselves in Heaven,
where neither moth nor rust destroy,
and where thieves neither break in nor steal.
For where your treasure is,
there will your heart be too.

In prayer we bring before the Lord our own needs and the needs of those we love. We take time to consider the needs of the world and intercede for those who do not or cannot pray. We offer petitions for the improvement of the human condition so that our world will be a better place to live, and all people may contribute to building up God's kingdom here on earth.

Intercessions

*G*ood and gracious Father, we thank you for your many blessings today. With confidence in your loving care we come to you at the close of this day to present our needs and the needs of all your people.

Response: *Lord, receive our prayer, through the intercession of St. Thérèse.*

Grant to Church leaders and all those who minister in your name the grace to lead lives of holiness, we pray. **R.**

Inspire world leaders to govern with integrity and justice, we pray. **R.**

Encourage and strengthen missionaries who preach the Gospel message and witness to your love for all peoples, we pray. **R.**

Give to parents the love, wisdom, and courage they need to form their children as disciples of your Son, we pray. **R.**

Bless all the children of the world with love and security, we pray. **R.**

Kindle in the hearts of young people the desire to follow a vocation to the religious life, we pray. **R.**

Comfort all those who suffer in mind, body, or spirit, we pray. **R.**

Console the brokenhearted, the troubled, and the abandoned, we pray. **R.**

Welcome all who have died into the joy of heaven, we pray. **R.**

(Add any other spontaneous intentions and your particular intentions for this novena.)

Conclude your intercessions by praying to our heavenly Father in the words Jesus taught us:

Our Father, who art in heaven…

Closing Prayer

All-loving God, receive our evening prayer. Bring us safely through the night and grant us a restful sleep so that with the coming of a new day we may serve you with renewed strength and joy. We ask this in the name of Jesus, your Son. Amen.

Mary, Jesus' Mother and ours, is always ready to intercede for those who ask her help.

Hail, Holy Queen, Mother of mercy, our life, our sweetness, and our hope! To you we cry, poor banished children of Eve; to you we send up our sighs, mourning and weeping in this valley of tears. Turn then, most gracious advocate, your eyes of mercy toward us, and after this our exile, show to us the blessed fruit of your womb, Jesus. O clement, O loving, O sweet Virgin Mary.

May God's blessing remain with us forever. In the name of the Father, and of the Son, and of the Holy Spirit. Amen.

Pauline
BOOKS & MEDIA

The Daughters of St. Paul operate book and media centers at the following addresses. Visit, call, or write the one nearest you today, or find us at www.pauline.org.

CALIFORNIA
3908 Sepulveda Blvd, Culver City, CA 90230   310-397-8676
3250 Middlefield Road, Menlo Park, CA 94025   650-562-7060

FLORIDA
145 S.W. 107th Avenue, Miami, FL 33174   305-559-6715

HAWAII
1143 Bishop Street, Honolulu, HI 96813   808-521-2731

ILLINOIS
172 North Michigan Avenue, Chicago, IL 60601   312-346-4228

LOUISIANA
4403 Veterans Memorial Blvd, Metairie, LA 70006   504-887-7631

MASSACHUSETTS
885 Providence Hwy, Dedham, MA 02026   781-326-5385

MISSOURI
9804 Watson Road, St. Louis, MO 63126   314-965-3512

NEW YORK
115 E. 29th Street, New York City, NY 10016   212-754-1110

SOUTH CAROLINA
243 King Street, Charleston, SC 29401   843-577-0175

TEXAS
No book center; for parish exhibits or outreach evangelization, contact:
210-569-0500, or SanAntonio@paulinemedia.com, or P.O. Box 761416,
San Antonio, TX 78245

VIRGINIA
1025 King Street, Alexandria, VA 22314   703-549-3806

CANADA
3022 Dufferin Street, Toronto, ON M6B 3T5   416-781-9131

¡También somos su fuente para libros,
videos y música en español!